Science Questions

Why Is the Sky Blue?

by Rebecca Pettiford

Bullfrog
Books

Ideas for Parents and Teachers

Bullfrog Books let children practice reading informational text at the earliest reading levels. Repetition, familiar words, and photo labels support early readers.

Before Reading
- Discuss the cover photo. What does it tell them?
- Look at the picture glossary together. Read and discuss the words.

Read the Book
- "Walk" through the book and look at the photos. Let the child ask questions. Point out the photo labels.
- Read the book to the child, or have him or her read independently.

After Reading
- Prompt the child to think more. Ask: The sky can look many different colors. What colors have you seen in the sky? Do you know why you've seen those colors?

Bullfrog Books are published by Jump!
5357 Penn Avenue South
Minneapolis, MN 55419
www.jumplibrary.com

Library of Congress Cataloging-in-Publication Data

Names: Pettiford, Rebecca, author.
Title: Why is the sky blue? / by Rebecca Pettiford.
Description: Minneapolis, MN: Jump!, Inc., [2023]
Series: Science questions | Includes index.
Audience: Ages 5–8
Identifiers: LCCN 2022011571 (print)
LCCN 2022011572 (ebook)
ISBN 9798885240598 (hardcover)
ISBN 9798885240604 (paperback)
ISBN 9798885240611 (ebook)
Subjects: LCSH: Sky—Color—Juvenile literature.
Meteorological optics—Juvenile literature.
Classification: LCC QC976.C6 P48 2023 (print)
LCC QC976.C6 (ebook)
DDC 551.56/6—dc23/eng20220517
LC record available at
https://lccn.loc.gov/2022011571
LC ebook record available at
https://lccn.loc.gov/2022011572

Editor: Jenna Gleisner
Designer: Emma Bersie

Photo Credits: ImagineDesign/Shutterstock, cover; chairoij/Shutterstock, 1; BLAGORODEZ/Shutterstock, 3; Serg64/Shutterstock, 4; Pakhnyushchy/Shutterstock, 5; Alexey Repka/Shutterstock, 6–7; Thoom/Shutterstock, 8, 23tl; Anna Pasichnyk/Shutterstock, 9; Melinda Nagy/Shutterstock, 10–11, 23bl; Net Vector/Shutterstock, 12; PANG WRP/Shutterstock, 13; Procy/Shutterstock, 14–15; Eric Mischke/iStock, 16–17, 23br; Freedom365day/Shutterstock, 18–19; jamesvancouver/iStock, 20–21; Nelli Covali/Dreamstime, 23tr; Boonchuay1970/Shutterstock, 24.

Printed in the United States of America at Corporate Graphics in North Mankato, Minnesota.

Table of Contents

Blue Light 4

Why We See Blue 22

Picture Glossary 23

Index 24

To Learn More 24

Blue Light

It is a sunny day.

The sky looks bright blue. Why?

The Sun shines on Earth.

The light moves in waves.

light waves

8

Sunlight looks white.

But it is all colors
of the rainbow.

It hits particles
in the air.

The light scatters.

We see colors!

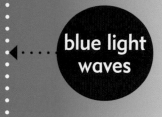
blue light
waves

Blue light waves are short.
They scatter the most.

We see blue!

13

At night, the sky looks black.

Why?

There isn't enough sunlight to see.

We see no color.

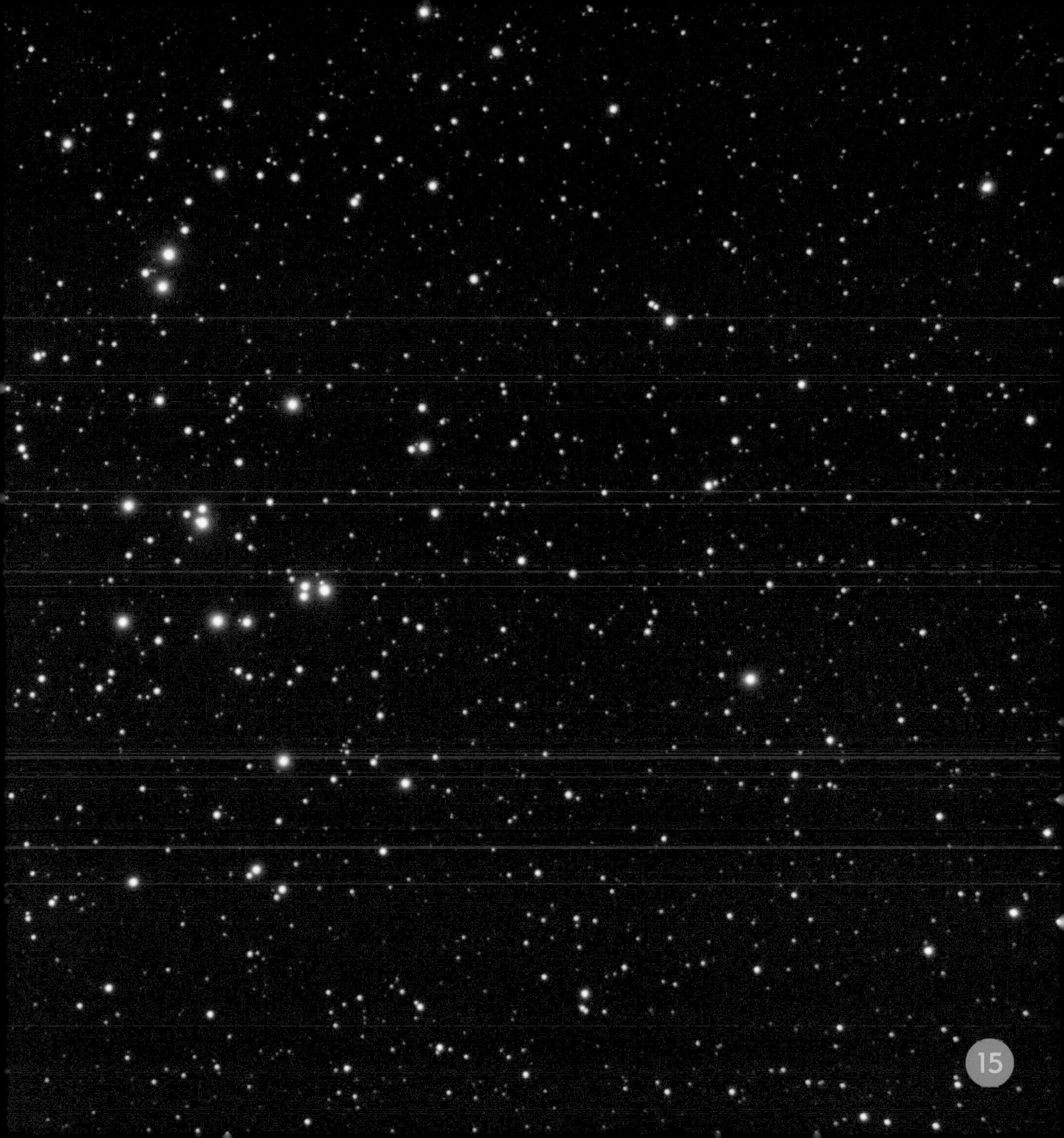

Look!

It is the sunrise.

The Sun is low in the sky.

It hits more particles.

We see longer
light waves.

We see pink, red,
and orange!

Look at the sky.

What colors do you see?

Why We See Blue

Blue light waves are short. They scatter more than other colors. This is why we see blue in the sky. Take a look!

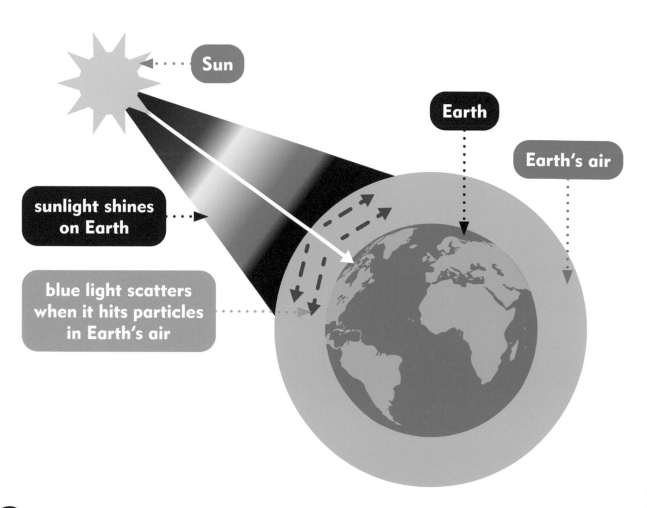

Sun

Earth

Earth's air

sunlight shines on Earth

blue light scatters when it hits particles in Earth's air

Picture Glossary

light waves
Rays of energy from the
Sun that move in waves.

particles
Very small pieces of matter,
such as dust.

scatters
Spreads out and moves
in different directions.

sunrise
The event in the morning
when the Sun first appears
above the horizon.

Index

air 11

blue 5, 12, 13

colors 11, 14, 21

Earth 7

light 8, 11, 12, 18

light waves 8, 12, 18

night 14

particles 11, 18

scatters 11, 12

Sun 7, 18

sunlight 9, 14

sunrise 17

To Learn More

Finding more information is as easy as 1, 2, 3.

❶ Go to www.factsurfer.com

❷ Enter "whyistheskyblue" into the search box.

❸ Choose your book to see a list of websites.

24